# This book belongs to

Abbey

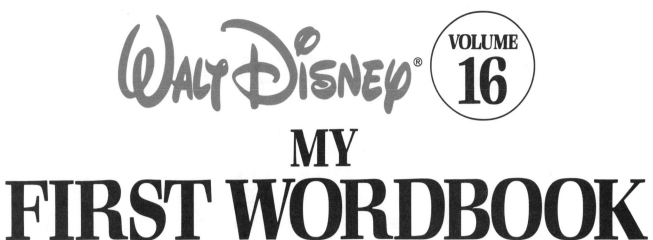

# Walt Disney®

VOLUME 16

# MY FIRST WORDBOOK

**WALT DISNEY FUN-TO-LEARN LIBRARY**

# Fun at the Playground

Listen! Did you know that every single person and every single thing in the whole world has a name? Big things? Little things? Here are some things Morty, Ferdie, Huey, Dewey, and Louie like best. Do you know their names?

slide

mud puddle

seesaw

tricycle

top

climbing bars

swing

drinking - fountain

ball

sandbox

bat

fort

doll

shovel

blocks

# People at Work

People who work have special names, too.
This firefighter has come just in time to save
Mickey's barbecue.

"Whew!" Mickey says. "I'm really glad to
see you!"

fire truck

hydrant

firefighter

hose

boots

barbecue grill

"Where's the nearest bank?" Uncle Scrooge asks the police officer who is directing traffic. "I want to make a small deposit."

"Th-that way, sir!" the officer exclaims. He can hardly believe what he sees in Scrooge's car.

Can you see some other people at work in this picture?

BANK

bus driver

passenger

bus

police officer

money

car

mailbag

mail carrier

# More People at Work

"Listen carefully, class," the teacher says. "This is a very important lesson."

Huey and Louie write down everything the teacher says. But what is Dewey doing? Do you think he hears what the teacher is saying?

clock

blackboard

teacher

map

globe

eraser

chalk

notebook

student

book

paper

desk

The doctor is giving Morty and Ferdie their checkups. "You are both just fine," she says. Morty scraped his knee. But he didn't cry at all!

scales

patient

bandage

examining table

doctor

"Open wide, please," says the dentist. But look at Goofy's teeth! The dentist doesn't know where to begin!

Does your dentist's office look like this one?

light

X-ray machine

dentist

teeth

drill

# At the Grocery Store

Goofy has a great idea. He's going to have a watermelon party.

"Please come, too," he tells the check-out clerk. "I'm going to invite everyone in town."

bottles

cans

oranges

watermelons

grocery cart

sign

Special Sale on watermelon

BUY AN EXTRA ONE!

check-out clerk

cash register

milk

bread

customer

# At the Restaurant

"Happy birthday, dear Goofy!" sing Mickey and the waitress and the cook. Mickey has invited Goofy for a birthday dinner at their favorite restaurant. The hamburgers are delicious, the sundaes are terrific—and the surprise birthday cake is the best of all.

cook

waitress

birthday cake

sundaes

glass

menu

hamburgers

spoon

tablecloth

fork

# Things That Go

**moving van**

"Stop!" Donald signals. Now the mother cat and her frisky kittens can cross the busy street. All around them are big machines that take people where they want to go. How many can you name?

**motorcycle**

**taxi**

**truck**

traffic lights

stop sign

STOP

school bus

POLICE

bicycle

police car

car

toy car

roller skates

# Things That Float

"I'm going to catch the biggest fish in the harbor," says Donald. But Uncle Scrooge isn't interested in catching a fish. He wants to bring home some oysters with pearls inside of them.

Uncle Scrooge and Donald have a rowboat. How many things that float do you see around them?

lighthouse

ocean liner

sailboat

cargo ship

ferry

tug boat

motorboat

yacht

ocean

buoy

rowboat

oars

# Things That Fly

Dumbo is the only flying elephant in the whole world. "I love to fly," says his friend Timothy Mouse. He hangs on tight to Dumbo and looks at all the flying machines in the sky.

"I'd like to try every one of them," says Timothy. "But I'm sure a flying elephant is the most fun."

balloon

airliner

light plane

blimp

glider

helicopter

bird

# Shapes and Colors

"Play ball!" shouts Mickey Mouse. He is up at bat for the All-Star team. Daisy Duck pitches for the True Hearts. She throws a fast ball, and Mickey swings.

"Hurrah for the All-Stars!" cheers the balloon man. "If they win, I'll fill the sky with my colored balloons."

Which colored balloon would you choose? How many different shapes do you see in the ball park?

diamond

square

rectangle

star

heart

blue

red

pink

orange

yellow

green

purple

triangle

circle

# Space

*Zooommm!* Super spacemen Goofy and Donald are off on another adventure. When they come back, they will have exciting stories to tell. Do you know the names of the things they can see from the window of their spaceship?

Donald is taking a walk in space. Watch out for that meteor, Donald!

helmet

space suit

meteor

# Our Earth

On a sunny day our earth looks bright and cheerful. Bees and butterflies are busy. Trees and flowers reach up toward the sun.

Dopey has a beautiful bouquet of flowers for Snow White. Be careful, Dopey! Those stones look slippery.

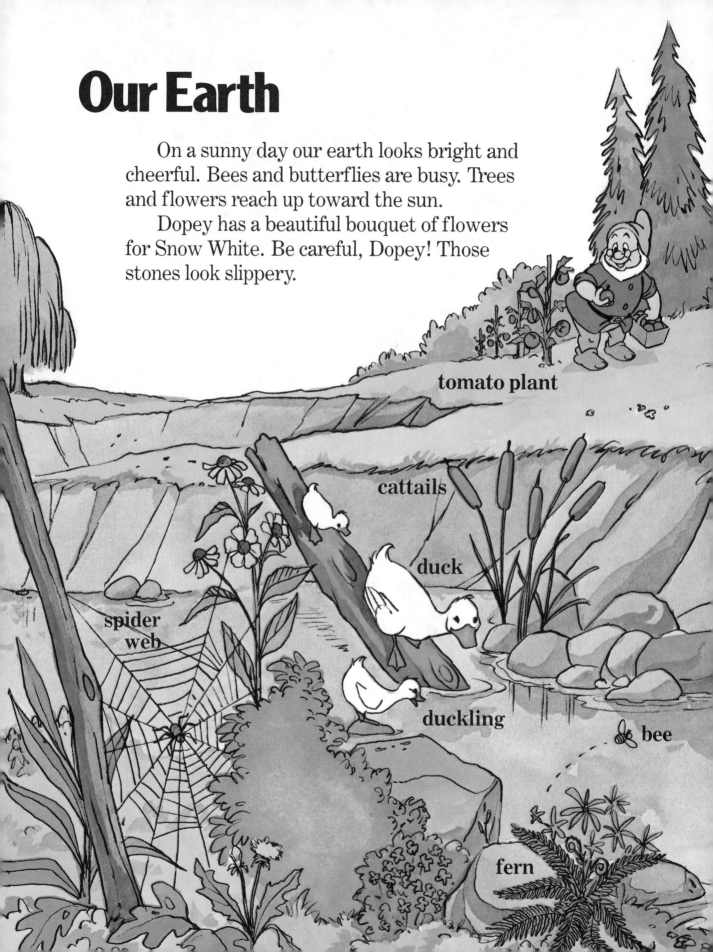

tomato plant

cattails

duck

spider web

duckling

bee

fern

scarecrow

onions

hoe

cabbage

spade

rake

tree

wild flowers

pool

turtle

bush

leaf

# Families

People have families who love them, and animals have families, too. Lady and Tramp and their puppies live with Jim Dear and Darling and their baby. They have wonderful times together.

"But goodness!" Darling exclaims. "Look at your puppies, Lady! I never saw babies so full of mischief!"

bookshelf

father

fireplace

armchair

footstool

puppy

slipper

newspaper

mother

picture

high chair

pillow

lamp

sofa

carpet

table

vase

teddy bear

baby

# On the Farm

"Where can that piglet be?" Grandma Duck wonders. She loves all the animals on her farm, but the baby pig is her favorite.

Crash! The billy goat is in a hurry to get his dinner. Watch out, Donald!

What are the other animals you see in the barnyard?

rooster

sheep

tractor

hat

goose

lamb

pig

piglet

# In the Jungle

Mowgli knows the animals that live in the jungle. Some of them are very big, and some of them are very fierce. Many are his friends. Today, Hathi the elephant is helping Mowgli take a cool bath in a jungle pool.

panther

banana tree

hippopotamus

pool

water lily

monkey

elephant

tiger

orangutan

snake

# Woodland Animals

"Watch me jump," Bambi tells his woodland friends.
"I like to jump, too," says Thumper the rabbit.
"The name of the game is leapfrog," says the frog.
Some of the animals would rather watch than play.
The skunk is busy smelling the flowers. Careful, skunk,
that bee is watching you! Do you know the names of all
the animals in the picture?

owl

cardinal

deer

rabbit

pigeon

skunk

frog

mouse

# At the Pet Show

Morty and Ferdie have entered Pluto in a
pet show. They hurry to get in line for the
judging. Do you know the names of all the pets
shown here?

Soon the judge chooses his favorite pets.

dog

turtle

hamster

goldfish

parrot

cat

Hurray! Pluto wins the blue ribbon! Who
has won the red ribbon? The yellow ribbon?
Is there a pet that you like best of all?

judge

collar

ribbon

# Under the Sea

Uncle Scrooge and Donald can't see what
is going on beneath their boat, but you can.
Name the sea creatures in this picture.

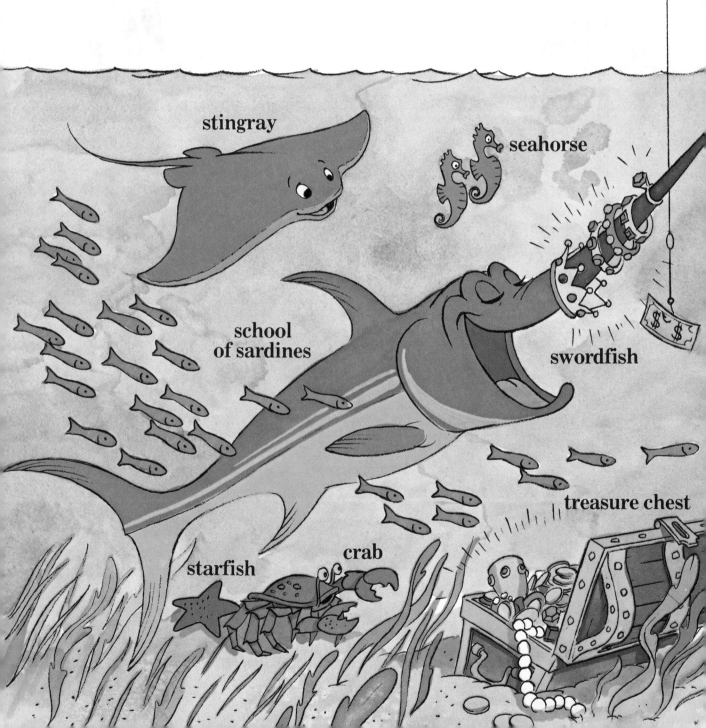

DAISY

jellyfish

whale

eel

turtle

porpoise

octopus

clam

seaweed

Every day, Christopher Robin uses his eyes and ears to see and hear the friends he likes best. Every day, they talk together and play games.

"Good morning, dear Pooh," says Christopher Robin. "Good morning, Rabbit." Then Christopher Robin and Rabbit stretch their legs and go for an early-morning run through the Hundred-Acre Wood.

shoulder

arm

knee

leg

ankle

foot

# Spring

"Spring, spring, sparkly spring!" sings Pooh. In the spring he plants his garden, and Kanga comes to help him clean house. Their friends are busy, too. It is nearly Easter, and Rabbit and Piglet are practicing for the Easter egg hunt. "Look what I've found," says Rabbit.

Tigger flies a kite. Little Roo gets out his jump rope and jumps thirty-one times without stopping.

mop

broom

pail

tulip

seeds

daffodil

trowel

flower pot

jump rope

kite

bird eggs

nest

Easter eggs

basket

# Summer

Summer is the time to swim and have fun. "Watch me dive!" shouts Donald. Huey hurries to swim out of his way.

Daisy and Louie set the table for a Fourth of July picnic lunch. The guests can watch the fireworks as they eat. Do you think Uncle Scrooge will wake up in time for the picnic?

cake

shovel

sand pail

pool

diving board

# Fall

**colored leaves**

When fall comes, it's time to think about Halloween fun. "Trick or treat! We love to eat!" shout Tigger, Piglet, and Rabbit.

Can you find the ghost, the cowboy, and the pirate in the picture? Pooh has jars of his best honey to put into their trick-or-treat bags.

**nut**

**squirrel**

**ghost**

**pirate**

**jack-o'-lantern**

**cowboy**

**rake**

One of the best things about fall is Thanksgiving. "I hope you're hungry!" says Minnie. She has roasted a big turkey for Thanksgiving dinner. She has cooked other good things, too. Do you see some of your favorite foods?

Mickey and Morty and Ferdie can hardly wait to start eating—and Pluto is ready, too!

coffee pot

pie

turkey

platter

corn

plate

rolls

mashed potatoes

apples

cup
saucer

squash

# Winter

*Brrrr!* It's winter now, with cold and snow and ice and wind. But Goofy doesn't care—today he is practicing his skating.

"We *like* winter," says Huey and Louie and Dewey. "We like snowstorms and snowmen and—most of all!—we love Christmas!"

gloves

ski cap

ice

ice skates

muffler

snowman

snowball

sparrow

Christmas tree

ornament

presents

snow

sled